IMAGES OF ENGLAND

SALTASH

IMAGES OF ENGLAND

SALTASH

JOAN RENDELL

TEMPUS

Frontispiece: An aerial view of Saltash.

First published 2004

Tempus Publishing Limited
The Mill, Brimscombe Port,
Stroud, Gloucestershire, GL5 2QG
www.tempus-publishing.com

© Joan Rendell, 2004

The right of Joan Rendell to be identified as the Author
of this work has been asserted in accordance with the
Copyrights, Designs and Patents Act 1988.

British Library Cataloguing in Publication Data.
A catalogue record for this book is available from the British Library.

ISBN 0 7524 3157 9

Typesetting and origination by Tempus Publishing Limited.
Printed in Great Britain by Midway Colour Print, Wiltshire.

Contents

A painting by Henry Martin showing the bottom of Albert Road, Saltash, in 1899. Martin was the first painter to work at Newlyn but he left West Cornwall for Plymouth in 1883, just as the 'Newlyn School' was being recognised. He later moved to Saltash, residing at No.6 Brunel Terrace (now Old Ferry Road). He died in 1908 and was buried in St Stephen's churchyard.

Acknowledgements

This volume has been made possible by the kind co-operation of Saltash Heritage Centre, Mr Colin Squires and Mr David Coles, who gave so freely of their knowledge and expertise to select and scan suitable subjects to make the book interesting, and to whom grateful thanks are extended. Thanks also for the loan of photographs, to Mrs 'Bill' Glanville and Mr John Neale.

Saltash Heritage Centre
Saltash Heritage was founded in 1986, and became a registered charity the following year. Its aims were: to promote interest in the history of Saltash and district, to make a collection of relevant material, and to provide a museum in the town.

Following the vacation of the ground floor of No.17 Lower Fore Street in 1999, Saltash Town Council leased the whole building to Saltash Heritage. Substantial grants were then obtained from the Heritage Lottery Fund and the Single Regeneration Budget Challenge Fund for the refurbishment of the premises and the creation of a museum on the ground floor. This project became a reality in the year 2000, resulting in Saltash Heritage being granted Full Registration status by the national museums body.

Today, the museum has a permanent display explaining Saltash's origins (a borough was founded in around 1175), and later events. Temporary displays deal with themes covering the civil parishes that make up the Saltash Postal District: Botusfleming, Landrake, Landulph, Pillaton, St Dominick, St Germans and St Mellion.

Saltash Heritage Centre
17 Lower Fore Street
Saltash
Cornwall
PL12 6JQ
www.saltash-heritage.org.uk

Introduction

There may be a tendency today to regard Saltash as a dormitory town for Plymouth, but never let Saltash people hear you say that! Saltash is Cornish and let no one forget it. Plymouth is a world away; the River Tamar is the great divide and what happens on its Devon or Plymouth side is nothing whatever to do with Saltash; when you are in the Duchy of Cornwall you are, as it were, on foreign soil, and Saltash is one of the gateways to that delectable part of the British Isles.

The town of Saltash is said to have been established by Anglo-Saxons from Wessex who became dominant in the area and created the ancient Passage across the Tamar estuary at Esse (pronounced 'Essa'), later known as Ash and then Saltash. The 1584 Charter of Elizabeth I says 'Essa is now commonly called Saltash'.

The town has seen plenty of battle action over the years, notably during the Civil War when the Cornish, who were loyal to the King, clashed with the Parliamentarians of Plymouth. As a result of this the town changed hands several times, taken first by one side and then the other. In 1549 Cornwall was in turmoil against the introduction of the Protestant litany, and in his little book, *A Glimpse of Saltash*, local historian Douglas C. Vosper says that many acts of barbarity were carried out at this time.

Even today, the view of Saltash seen from the Devon side of the river gives hints of an ancient town, its houses ascending a steep hill with its church at the top, and at its foot, perhaps incongruously, a public house painted as the Union flag – certainly an eye-catcher for all travellers crossing the rail or road bridges! Dominating all is the mighty Royal Albert Bridge. Although it now has a companion in the modern Tamar road bridge it still stands proudly as master of all, rising 100ft above the Tamar.

A ferry across the river has existed since time immemorial; indeed the very birth of Saltash itself could have come from the river trade. It has been said that most Saltash men are connected with the water in one way or another; many still join the navy and many were and still are employed at Devonport Dockyard, in older days engaged on shipbuilding. Ships and the sea are in the blood of Saltash men.

Today the town is busy and outgoing, and has grown considerably in size in recent years. It boasts every amenity and the traffic streams unendingly across the Tamar road bridge by day and by night, but it retains its individuality – and its Cornishness.

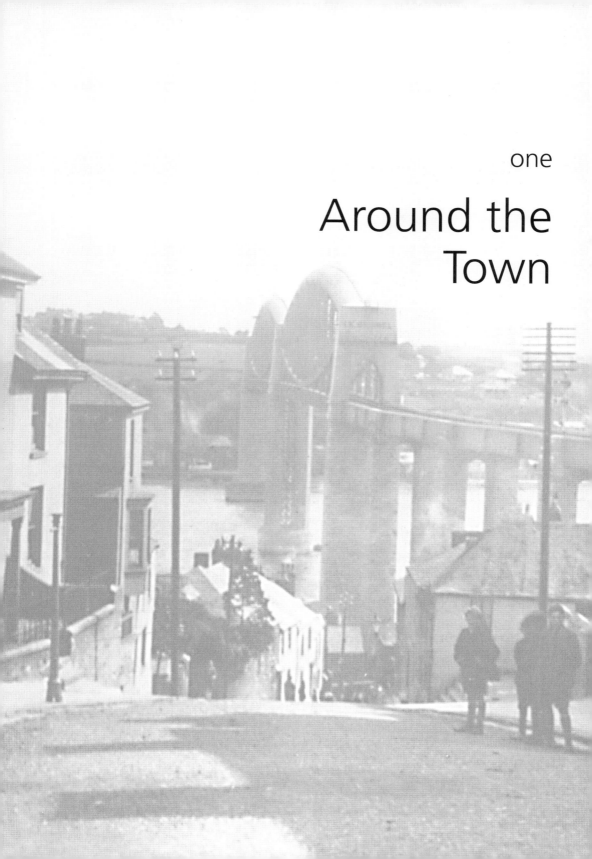

one

Around the Town

An unusual view of Saltash railway station and the Tamar road bridge, which in this case is eclipsing the Royal Albert Bridge, over which a long train (probably from London) is passing.

King George VI and Queen Elizabeth (later The Queen Mother) arrived at Saltash railway station on 12 July 1950, *en route* to the Royal Cornwall Show, being held at Kelly Bray, near Callington. The King and Queen are seen here being greeted by the Mayor and Mayoress of Saltash, Alderman George Deacon and Mrs Deacon. Town Clerk Mr Gordon Bellingham is standing at the right.

Princess Margaret accompanied her parents on their visit to Cornwall on 12 July 1950 and they are seen leaving Saltash railway station before being driven away in the royal Daimler.

Princess Margaret attended an exhibition in Munich, Germany in 1973 and is seen here inspecting a display which includes Saltash's two silver ceremonial oar maces. One of the maces is dated 1623. They are the oldest such maces extant in Britain and symbolise Saltash Borough's jurisdiction over the Liberty of the Water Tamar, which had its origin in medieval times, its last vestiges being abolished as recently as 1901.

Left: Prince Philip flew to Wearde School on 18 May 1978 to see the progress of East Cornwall participants in his Duke of Edinburgh Award Scheme. He piloted the helicopter himself and is seen leaving it on his arrival.

Below: On his visit to Wearde School on 18 May 1978 the Duke of Edinburgh is seen talking to members of a Saltash group. From left to right are: Jeremy Bodman, Amanda Randall, Mrs Liz Sharpe (instructor) and Peter Whitfield.

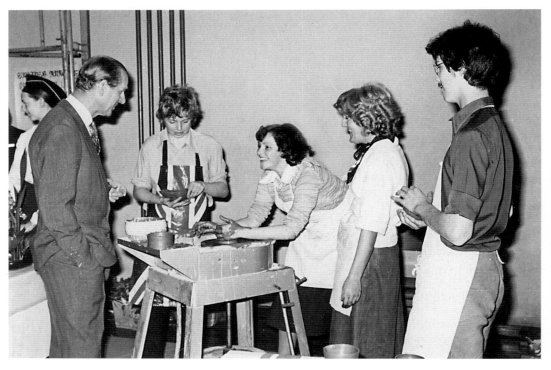

The Royal Train brought Queen Elizabeth II and the Duke of Edinburgh to Saltash on 25 July 1962 at the start of a tour of Duchy of Cornwall estates and farms. The Queen included Landulph in her tour, after visiting Duchy tenant Mr Kellock Roberts and his wife Eileen at Landulph Farm. She walked down the lane to the parish church and is here seen escorted by Mr J.B. (Jock) Stanier, Duchy Land Steward. The Duke is following them.

The Accession of King Edward VII, being proclaimed at Waterside by the Mayor of Saltash in January 1901. Behind the crowd is Ashtor House which contained a refreshment room and a hall. It was demolished in 1938 in order to widen the ferry approach.

A Black Prince Pageant was held in the grounds of Trematon Castle (where the Black Prince lived) on 7 and 8 July 1914. The scenes for the pageant were set in the year 1362, the script was written by Revd William Diggens, vicar of St Stephen by Saltash, and over 200 people took part in it.

Part of the large cast of the Black Prince Pageant in 1914, just before the outbreak of the First World War.

Above: The procession celebrating King George V's Silver Jubilee, led by Saltash Working Men's Band, returns along Callington Road from the Recreation Field at Longstone on 6 May 1935. On the right, the first two houses still exist; the third, Well Park, was demolished to make way for the new Wesley Chapel (the fourth!) in 1988.

Opposite above: The Arch House was one of the oldest features of Saltash. Its site was in line with the present day HSBC Bank premises. The portion spanning the street was demolished in 1859 so that loaded wagons could reach the new railway station from the western approaches to the town. Wesley Road, King Edward Road and Essa Road did not then exist. Demolition work was imminent when this photograph was taken – the windows had already been removed in preparation.

Opposite below: In Fore Street, to mark Queen Victoria's Diamond Jubilee in 1897, a Jubilee archway of foliage was erected alongside Gate House (a protruding building demolished two years later). The arch bore a 'VR' monogram and a shield on which local artist Alfred Snell painted a three-masted ship at anchor, copied from one of the ancient Borough seals. At the left is the Commercial Hotel (now The Brunel), and the entrance to its yard, now the site of two shops.

Above: The entrance to an ice-house in the garden of Alexandra House, Station Road shortly before it was demolished in 1962. An ice-house was the equivalent of a modern refrigerator. Each winter the chamber was packed with crushed ice and insulated with straw. The ice usually lasted throughout the year and was used for keeping food fresh, cooling drinks, etc.

Opposite: Early in the twentieth century, the Slade Tea Gardens were a popular venue, both for outings and for leisurely meals in pleasant surroundings. The gardens extended from North Road to New Road (now Old Ferry Road). The house in which the food was prepared still exists; it was later named 'St Gabriel's' and is now No.86 North Road.

Above: Mary Newman's Cottage, Culver Road, *c.* 1920. Apart from its supposed association with Mary Newman, Sir Francis Drake's first wife, the building is of great intrinsic interest. Its basic structure is of a late-medieval date. Undoubtedly it is the oldest dwelling remaining in the town.

Left: Mary Newman's Cottage is reputed to have been the home of Mary Newman, first wife of Sir Francis Drake. It was restored in recent times by the Tamar Protection Society and is open to the public. Mary Newman is buried in the church at St Budeaux, just across the river in Plymouth; it is also the church in which she was married.

North Road under snow, *c.* 1910. The two shops are Essa Cycle and Gun works (where petrol was also sold, in cans) and A. Irwin, baker. The shops and nine of the terraced houses were demolished in 1960 to make way for the Tamar road bridge approach road.

The Rustic Tea Gardens were created in around 1906 by Mr Frederick Newberry in a disused quarry near Sand Quay. They were entered through the archway of a former warehouse which was embellished with fancy timber work. On the hillside above can be seen a gazebo in the grounds of 'Rosecliffe', a large house in Lower Fore Street.

The origin of the Rustic Tea Gardens' name is apparent from this photograph! Amusements were provided as well as refreshments. The creator and proprietor of the Gardens, Mr Newberry, is seen here. Following his suicide the Gardens closed in the mid-1920s. In the early 1930s, Daw's Creamery utilised the premises. The Daw's Court residential apartments, Old Ferry Road, now stand on the site.

From 1893 to 1923 Saltash's post office was situated in what is today the lower half of Lloyds TSB Bank in Fore Street. In this photograph from about 1910 the entire staff (except the Postmaster, Mr Fred Rawling) is standing outside the premises. The two young boys were presumably messengers, who delivered telegrams etc.

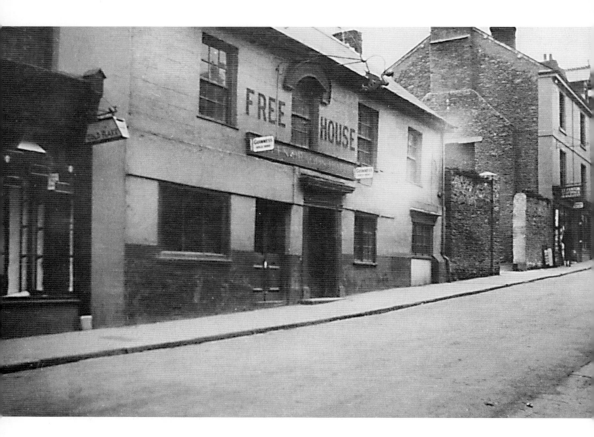

Above: The Green Dragon Hotel, once Saltash's principal coaching inn, was demolished in 1935 to make way for the Saltash Co-operative Society building. Next to the inn can be seen the entrance to the large yard which contained stables and a smithy; it is now the Culver Road car park. High over the doorway is the Green Dragon sign which was transferred to the present building.

Opposite above: Looking up Fore Street from the North Road junction, *c.* 1905. The junction was known as Simon's Corner – from the grocer's shop on the right. At the left-hand edge is the Railway Hotel, which is still there. Judging by all the citizens posing for it, the camera was then still a novelty!

Opposite below: Mrs Wilcox and her son or daughter (difficult to tell which!), standing outside her husband's grocery shop on the northern side of Fore Street, *c.* 1920. In relation to the present-day building line, the shop's site is in the middle of the roadway, just below Barclays Bank.

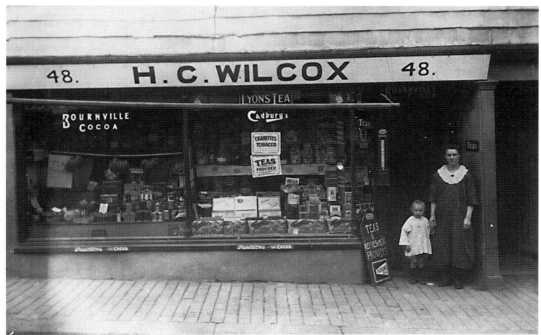

Left: No.9 Tamar Street, *c.* 1905, with Betsy Pope at the window of her shellfish shop. At the time there were many such shops at Waterside, their speciality being cockles. The granite door arch dated 1584 was preserved when this building was demolished in 1961 and was later incorporated in a new dwelling on the opposite side of the street.

Below: No.105 Fore Street in 1938. This seventeenth-century building was jettied, i.e. had an overhanging first floor. For many years it was Widdecombe's Bakery, where the world-famous(!) Saltash biscuit was made. When this photograph was taken it was occupied by Goad's upholstery. Tragically, the building was destroyed in the 1941 blitz and two occupants lost their lives.

After opening the Tamar Bridge on 26 April 1962, the Queen Mother attended a reception in the Guild Hall, where she was presented with a 20lb block of butter made at Daw's Creamery – the town's main industry – by nine-year-old Peter Bellingham. The butter was shaped to replicate the Great Common Seal surrounded by roses. Peter is being thanked by the Queen Mother, watched by his father, Mr Gordon Bellingham, the Town Clerk.

Above: Captain J.B. Nicholson, Saltash's Chief Air-Raid Warden during the Second World War, stands outside the Masonic Hall, Lower Fore Street, on a gas-mask issuing day in 1939.

Opposite: The Masonic Hall in Lower Fore Street was originally the town's first Methodist Chapel, built in 1808. It was acquired by the Zetland Lodge of Freemasons in 1892 after a new chapel was built in Upper Fore Street, adjoining the present-day Wesley Road. It is seen here before the façade was altered in around 1920. The building was demolished in 1959 to make way for the Tamar road bridge.

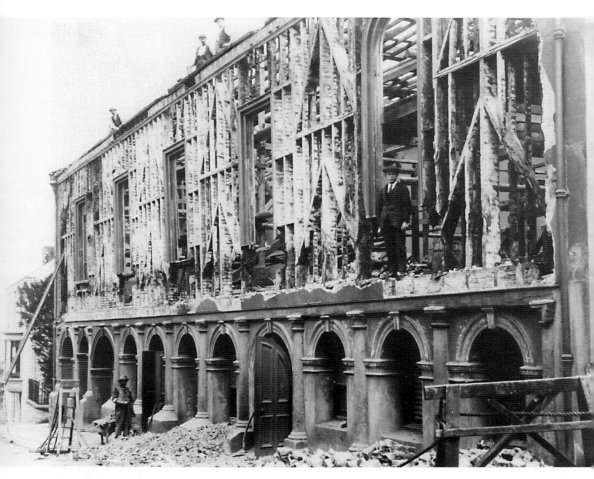

A major renovation of Saltash Guildhall took place in 1924. The first floor was rebuilt and the western end was remodelled, incorporating a new main entrance.

Looking down Fore Street, *c.* 1905. The Commercial Hotel (now The Brunel) is on the right. All the buildings on the left-hand side have gone, due partly to German bombing in 1941 and partly to road widening and redevelopment commencing in the 1960s.

Looking up Lower Fore Street, 1912. The large house on the right is 'Rosecliffe', and higher up on the same side is the Masonic Hall. These properties and all in between were demolished in 1959 to make way for the Tamar road bridge. The footway cobblestones were removed in 1921.

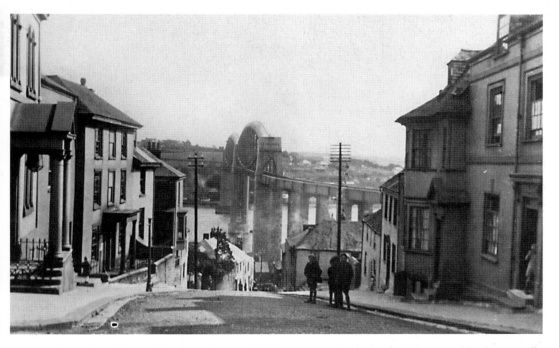

Looking down Lower Fore Street, c. 1925. The view now includes the Tamar road bridge as well as the Royal Albert railway bridge but the street is as steep as ever!

Left: The Mansion, off Fore Street, in 1968. This eighteenth-century house was acquired by Saltash Working Men's Club at the end of the Second World War as a replacement for premises destroyed in the 1941 blitz. The site was affected by the route of the Saltash bypass, so the building was demolished in 1985.

Below: Apple Tree Cottage, Forder, was the best-known of the Saltash area's tea and pleasure gardens. From early in the nineteenth century until 1938, it was a popular destination for day-trippers. Many used the frequent train service from Plymouth and walked from Saltash station, while others arrived by boat at Forder Creek. The thatch was removed from the roof in 1900.

Victoria Gardens.

Saltash near Plymouth.

Saltash, Tamar Street

Above: Victoria Gardens, Saltash, *c.* 1910. The gardens were created to mark Queen Victoria's Diamond Jubilee in 1897. The imposing obelisk was erected by public subscription to commemorate Major General Sir William Penn Symons, of Hatt House near Saltash, who was mortally wounded eight days after the Boer War began in 1899.

Left: Tamar Street, looking south from its junction with Albert Road, *c.* 1905. Butcher Cory's shop is on the corner. Mr Cory is posing in his doorway but the lady in the foreground seems totally unaware of the camera.

Tamar Street — Saltash

A busy scene at the northern end of Tamar Street, in around 1905. Pictured outside his shop, Andrew Pope junior is carrying a basket of fruit. On the left is the striped pole denoting the barber's shop of Ernest Hitchens. All these properties were demolished in 1961, except part of the Passage House Inn, later renamed The Boatman.

This building which once stood in North Road, Saltash, was erected in 1872 as a Board School following the 1870 Education Act. It was later brought into the elementary education system and was popularly known as the Council School, catering for over 600 infants, boys and girls. Badly damaged by fire in 1975, it was eventually demolished prior to excavation work for the Saltash Tunnel approach.

two

Bridge, River and Ferry

The third stream-powered floating bridge at Saltash Ferry. This vessel, in service from 1866 to 1891, was the last to have a wooden superstructure. Engineman Richard Ellery is standing on the prow.

The first all-steel vessel for the Saltash Ferry. Built by Willoughby Brothers of Plymouth for Saltash Borough Council, it was brought into service in 1891. Here, foot passengers are seen coming ashore on the Devon side, vehicular traffic having been allowed off first.

In 1896 the Saltash Ferry required major repairs. While it was out of service, a raft-like barge fitted with hinged ramps was employed, tied alongside a steamer. This substitute was quite small so that the wagon and four seen here make a full load!

Men on an outing in around 1910 are seen disembarking from the Saltash Ferry on the Devon side. They are all wearing distinctive white Panama hats and buttonholes, but it is not known what organisation they were representing: could it have been a bowling club?

Above: Soon after the start of the First World War, an army encampment was made in fields on the outskirts of Saltash. The main unit stationed there was the 3rd Battalion, King's Own Royal Lancaster Regiment. One company set off for France on 17 November 1914, monopolising the Saltash Ferry as they departed.

Opposite above: In this photograph taken in 1911, a new ferry vessel has just arrived from the builders and is moored on the Devon side before being put into service. Alongside is the temporary 'horse-boat', used whenever its predecessor broke down! Saltash Passage is in the background.

Opposite below: A circus wagon leaves the Saltash Ferry, around 1912. Every type of traffic was carried on the ferry; it had to be, otherwise a long detour had to be made in order to get across the river.

Above: The first underwater electricity cable being laid across the Tamar, *c.* 1929.

Opposite above: The sailing barge *Flora May* passing Saltash Ferry, *c.* 1914. She was built at Stonehouse in 1897 for Capt. Charlie Dymond of St Budeaux and she was used to carry bricks to Camel's Head, grain to (and flour from) Budshead Mill, and roadstone from the Lynher River quarries.

Opposite below: Saltash Ferry, *c.* 1950. Steam ferry No.6 was built by Philip of Dartmouth and replaced its predecessor in 1927. Originally designed to accommodate three rows of vehicles, it was widened in 1938 to take an extra row. It was this vessel that made the final crossing before the closure of the service in October 1961.

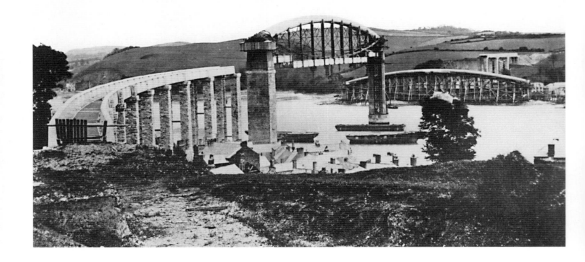

Above: The Royal Albert Bridge in around 1890, with Brunel's broad gauge track clearly visible. Note the fields and countryside views on the right, now almost entirely built over.

Opposite above: A crowd gathered to witness the ceremonial last crossing of Saltash Ferry on 24 October 1961. It was an emotional occasion and dry eyes were in the minority!

Opposite below: The second truss of the Royal Albert Bridge is under construction on the Devon shore in this mid–1858 photograph. In the foreground, the site of Saltash railway station has been excavated.

A general view of Saltash in about 1900. A century later, most of the river and waterfront features have gone – the paddle steamers, the ferry and the buildings. Only Brunel's Royal Albert Bridge, completed in 1859, remains unchanged apart from the addition of bracings to the main trusses.

Above: The beach at Waterside, 20 August 1900. On the left is the Church of the Good Shepherd, a Church of England mission provided for the people of Waterside in 1895. In 1945 the building was taken over by the Saltash Boys' Club. Redevelopment of Waterside was carried out in stages from 1957 to 1964. However, two-and-a-half public houses were spared, including the Union Inn, seen centre. This building is now painted as one huge Union flag and is the most conspicuous sight of Saltash as one crosses by train or road from the Devon side.

Opposite above: This postcard shows the precursor of the present Saltash Pier, in around 1908. At its extremity it had a floating pontoon known as a 'dummy' on which was a shelter for passengers awaiting the arrival of the steamboats operating the regular ferry service to Devonport. Upstream from the Royal Albert Bridge, the industrial training ship for boys, *Mount Edgcumbe* can be seen. She was moored there from 1877 to 1920.

Opposite below: Messrs Jefford Bros, the operators of Tor Quarry at Burraton Coombe, owned a number of sailing barges to deliver roadstone to customers. Here are two of the fleet at Saltash Passage, around 1910.

Above: The Mayor of Saltash,
Alderman T. Stanlake, unveils a
plaque to commemorate the
centenary of the opening of the
Royal Albert Bridge, at Saltash
railway station on the 1 May 1959.
In 1977 the plaque was moved to
the St Budeaux end of the bridge.

Right: With the opening of the
Tamar Bridge, a bust of Isambard
Kingdom Brunel was erected in a
prominent position by the
roundabout at the end of the
bridge.

The Royal Albert Bridge floodlit for its Centenary in 1959. In the foreground is the former Mission Church of the Good Shepherd (Church of England), then being used by the Saltash Boys' Club.

Mid-1961, during a short period when all three methods of crossing the Tamar from Saltash to St Budeaux could be seen together. The ferry made its last public run on 23 October 1961 and the Tamar Bridge opened for traffic the following day.

The granite columns of the Royal Albert Bridge are embedded in the solid rock, ninety feet below the water.

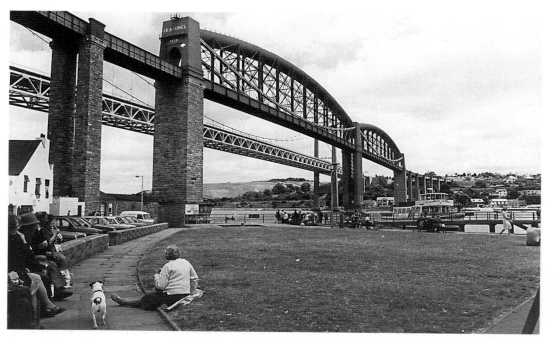

Groups of people wait to board steamers to take them on a pleasure cruise up the Tamar to Calstock in the 1980s.

The ferry, packed to capacity, arriving on the Devon side of the Tamar in 1964.

The Saltash Ferry arrives on the Devon side of the Tamar in 1964. Foot passengers are waiting to board for the return to Saltash. A second ferry is tied up in the far bottom right of the picture.

Members and officials of Saltash Borough Council assembled outside the Guildhall for the Royal Albert Bridge centenary celebrations on 1 May 1959. The Mayor, Alderman Tom Stanlake, is at the centre of the group.

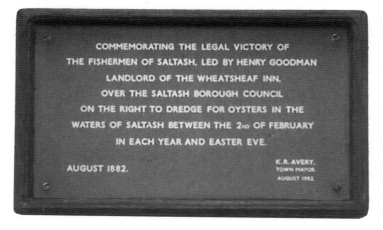

COMMEMORATING THE LEGAL VICTORY OF
THE FISHERMEN OF SALTASH, LED BY HENRY GOODMAN
LANDLORD OF THE WHEATSHEAF INN.
OVER THE SALTASH BOROUGH COUNCIL
ON THE RIGHT TO DREDGE FOR OYSTERS IN THE
WATERS OF SALTASH BETWEEN THE 2ND OF FEBRUARY
IN EACH YEAR AND EASTER EVE.

AUGUST 1882.

K.R. AVERY.
TOWN MAYOR.
AUGUST 1982.

A plaque on the wall outside the Wheatsheaf Inn on the Waterfront commemorates the legal victory of the fishermen of Saltash, led by Henry Goodman, landlord of the Wheatsheaf Inn, over Saltash Borough Council on the right to dredge for oysters in the waters of Saltash between 2 February each year and Easter Eve, in August 1882.

The Waterside Inn is a popular venue for day trippers to Saltash, and those waiting for steamers.

The HMS *Defiance* torpedo school was based on hulks moored in the Lynher estuary off Wearde Quay from 1886 to 1930. The establishment took its name from the 'wooden wall' seen here on the right. In 1896, Capt. Henry Jackson (later Sir Henry Jackson) made a series of pioneering radio transmissions from the ship and so became the first Briton to use radio for practical communication. Subsequently, radio instruction courses were held on HMS *Defiance*. In this photograph from about 1910 the masts have been extended to support aerials.

The paddle steamer *Empress* was one of a fleet operated by successive Saltash steamboat companies for seventy years from 1858. The vessels were used for regular passenger ferry and market produce services, as well as the excursion trade which reached phenomenal levels during the period 1880-1914.

Industrial training ship *Mount Edgcumbe* was moored off Saltash from 1877 to 1920. Managed by a charity, the vessel accommodated 200 boys at a time. Mostly orphans and minor offenders, they were given instruction relevant to naval careers. Beyond the ship in this 1910 photograph are some of the commercial premises which once lined the Saltash waterfront.

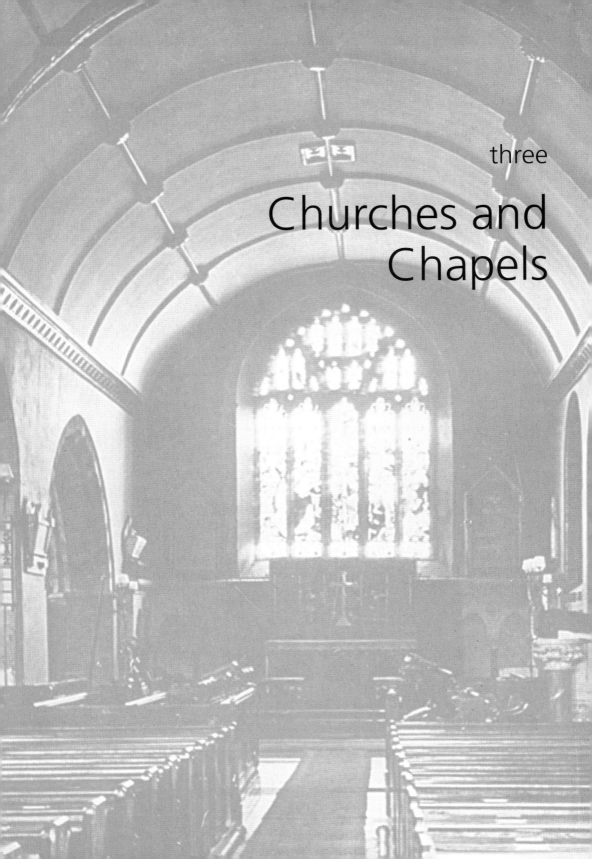

three

Churches and Chapels

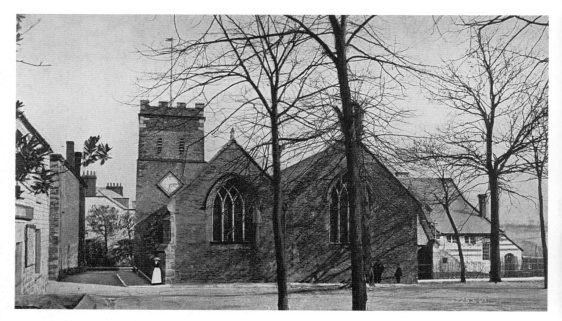

The parish church dedicated to Saints Nicholas and Faith, photographed around 1910. Although this is basically a twelfth-century building, until 1881 its status was that of a chapel of ease for Saltash Borough. To the right in the photograph is the church hall and ancillary rooms erected in 1897 to the design of the notable architect, Edmund H. Sedding.

The interior of SS Nicholas and Faith church, *c.* 1925. In the right-hand wall, two round-headed Norman arches can be seen. The nearest of these is the original south doorway (blocked up in the nineteenth century); the other leads to the south transept.

SS Nicholas and Faith church, *c.* 1935. A restoration funded by Mayor Drury's revivals of the 'Ancient Fair' in 1930 and 1931 had been completed. The work included the replacement of the battlements on the Norman tower with a more appropriate parapet.

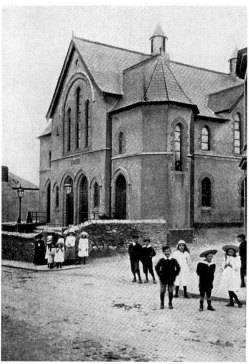

Above: The bells of SS Nicholas and Faith's church ready for re-hanging following the re-casting of the third bell from left, 1960.

Left: Wesley Chapel No.2 in Upper Fore Street opening in 1891. The area on its flank, not seen in this view of about 1900, is now Wesley Road. Note the children's fashions of the day – especially the wide-brimmed hat of the boy in right foreground!

Left: In 1908 the front of Wesley Chapel No.2 was refaced. Limestone blocks were used, together with Bath stone for the door and window arches. Sadly, the building was gutted by incendiary bombs during the 1941 blitz. Eventually a post office (successively the town's sixth) was built on the site.

Below: A harvest festival display, Saltash Wesley Chapel, 1910. These elaborate displays were a feature of Wesleyan (or Methodist) chapels at the time, and even the smallest country chapel put on a big show with fruit, vegetables, flowers, corn and often bread baked in the shape of a sheaf of corn.

Wesley Chapel No.3! This brick building in Glebe Avenue was opened in 1953. In 1989 it was superseded by the present chapel at the corner of Glebe Avenue and Callington Road.

Saltash Wesley Choir with the Mayor and Mayoress of Saltash, Alderman and Mrs William Gallagher, during a concert at the Wesley Chapel, Easter 1971. Sitting beside the Mayor is Revd Henry Carr, superintendent minister, and sitting beside the Mayoress is Mr Lancelot Parkes, the choirmaster.

A Saltash Wesley Sunday school outing to Mount Edgcumbe in around 1930, with Lance Parkes at the centre rear.

One of the stalls at a Saltash Toc H Fête at Longstone recreation field, 1950. On the right are Mr Gordon Bellingham (Town Clerk) his wife Muriel and their twin daughters.

Originally a barn, this building in Fore Street was converted to a Salvation Army Barracks and was eventually demolished to make way for YMCA premises erected in 1909-10. To the left, the back of Belle Vue Terrace can be seen.

four

People in the
News

Ferdinand Keast was appointed one of Saltash's two sergeants-at-mace in 1846. He became the senior town sergeant a few years later and took up residence in the Old Guildhall, where he remained in office and carried on his trade as a tailor until his death on New Year's Day, 1891. His nickname, known to all, was 'Nandy'.

One of Nandy's duties was as keeper of the borough jail (known as the Black Hole) on the ground floor of the Old Guildhall. He was also responsible for enforcing Saltash's jurisdiction over the 'Liberty of the Water Tamar', apprehending persons committing offences such as stealing, and mutinous conduct on board vessels.

Ferdinand Keast was a good-humoured man, and exercised tact in dealing with wrongdoers. But, if necessary, he was quick to administer a rap with his truncheon and follow it up with a head butt. He was very proud of his cranium, and would demonstrate its toughness by cracking a brazil nut against a doorstop with the back of his head! That was just one of those idiosyncrasies that made Nandy a popular character in Saltash.

May 1950 and the newly-elected Mayor of Saltash, Alderman George Deacon, stands outside the Guildhall with his Deputy (Councillor Cyril Underhill), the Town Clerk (Mr Gordon Bellingham), their spouses and the mace bearers.

Saltash's first woman Mayor was elected in 1952. Councillor Miss Winifred M. Fearnside was a Plymouth schoolteacher who resided in Saltash. She is well remembered for taking great interest in council housing. She is seen here presiding over a meeting of Saltash Borough council. From left to right at the table are: Mr Colin Badder (Borough Treasurer), Mr Colin Bellingham (Town Clerk), the Mayor, Alderman George Deacon (Deputy Mayor). In the foreground: Alderman Fred Smith, Councillor John Bidgood, Councillor James Down, and Alderman Harry Roden.

Above: Remembrance Day parade, 1949. The Mayor is Councillor Cyril E. Underhill.

Opposite above: Honorary Freemen of the Borough of Saltash. The existing Freemen – from left to right, Dr H.J. Hewitt, Mr C.C. Badder and Mr A.G. Bellingham – congratulate their newly-admitted colleague, Miss Winifred Fearnside, in February 1974. Dr Hewitt was Headmaster of Saltash County School from its opening in 1927 to 1952. It was renamed Saltash Grammar School in 1946. Mr Colin Badder was a former Borough Treasurer and Mr Gordon Bellingham was Town Clerk from 1949–1974.

Opposite below: The Fore Street entrance to the Guildhall in 1908, two years before the ground floor (earlier a pannier market) was closed. Flanked by the mace-bearers are, from left to right: Mr Frederick E. Cleverton (Town Clerk), Mr Richard Miller (Mayor), and Canon Arthur Preedy (Vicar of Saltash).

Mr Lance Parkes in costume for his role in the St Nicholas Amateur Operatic Society's production of *The Gondoliers* at the Drill Hall, Saltash in 1938. Mr Parkes was well known in musical circles in Saltash, being choirmaster of the Wesley Choir for a number of years. He served in the Royal Navy, retiring with the rank of Lieutenant and later became an Assistant Commissioner for National Savings in south-east and north Cornwall.

Saltash Scouts enjoying a meal they had prepared themselves whilst at camp, in around 1960.

During the Second World War, baby shows were popular events providing relief from the daily grind. The Mayor of Saltash, Councillor J.F. Ashton, is seen here with the infants and proud mothers who took part in a show held in 1942. In the background is Mrs Ellen Richards's drapery (now the Kashmir Balti House) in Lower Fore Street.

Saltash Boys' School class, *c.* 1910

Saltash Infants' School class, *c.* 1935. How well-behaved the children seem, and how serious they all look!

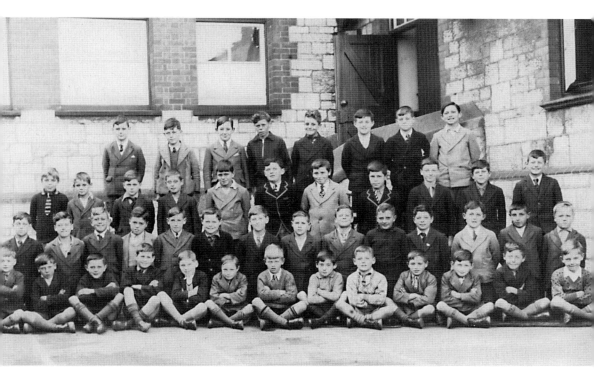

Saltash Boys' School class, 1936.

In 1971, pupils at Saltash Comprehensive School, Wearde, presented the play *Captain Noah and His Floating Zoo*, with this striking set.

A presentation to mark the retirement of Mr Ralph Crow, the Headmaster of Saltash Comprehensive (formerly Grammar) School from 1952 to 1973. Pictured from left to right: Miss Morwenna Jones (Senior Mistress), Mr Howard Moyse (Head of English), Mr Crow, Mr Ronald Castleton (Deputy Head), Mrs Crow, Mr Cyril Underhill (Chairman of Governors) Mr Michael Derges (Chairman of the PTA) and Professor David Coombes (a former Head Boy).

Above: The annual Saltash Co-operative Society Tea at Longstone Recreation Field, in 1908. The photograph is taken looking east, with the rear of Longstone Cottage and Prospect Cottage (now demolished), in the background.

Right: In August 1931 the well-known actor Cyril Maude (right) was invited to Saltash by the Mayor (his friend) Lt Col W.P. Drury to formally open the second revival of the 'Ancient Fair'. William Price Drury CBE was a Royal Marines officer who was also a prolific novelist and playwright. He was Mayor of Saltash 1929-1931, being one of the very few not elected from the membership of the borough council. During this Mayoralty he revived the Ancient Fair in order to raise funds for the restoration of St Nicholas's church.

Above: The 1950 or '51 annual dance of the Saltash branch of the National Farmers' Union was held in Satlash Guildhall. The Mayor and Mayoress, Alderman and Mrs George Deacon, were guests of honour.

Opposite above: The ancient ceremony of 'Beating the Bounds' to confirm the boundary of the Borough of Saltash was performed in 1951. Town Clerk Mr Gordon Bellingham had the dubious honour of being 'bumped' on the boundary stone at Notter Bridge.

Opposite below: To ensure that he would remember the course of the borough boundary at Notter Bridge, a youth received a ducking in the River Lynher!

The 2nd Saltash Wolf Cubs in camp at Stoketone in the early 1960s. At the centre of the back row is Cub Mistress Audrey Miller, and at the extreme right is Assistant Cub Mistress Joy Nodder.

William Odgers, VC (1834-1873). Falmouth-born William Odgers joined the Royal Navy in 1852 and married a Saltash girl soon afterwards. During the Maori Wars, while serving in HMS *Niger* he won the Victoria Cross at Waireka Hill, near New Plymouth, in 1860. It was the first Victoria Cross awarded for a deed on New Zealand soil. Odgers was invalided out in 1868, having reached the rank of Admiral's coxswain. He returned to Saltash and was the licensee of the Union Inn at Waterside until his death. His grave is in St Stephen's churchyard.

An early motor car, carrying a group of parliamentary election canvassers, moving off from New Road, Saltash in 1906. In the background is the arched entrance to Newberry's Rustic Tea Gardens. This length of New Road was renamed Old Ferry Road in 1969.

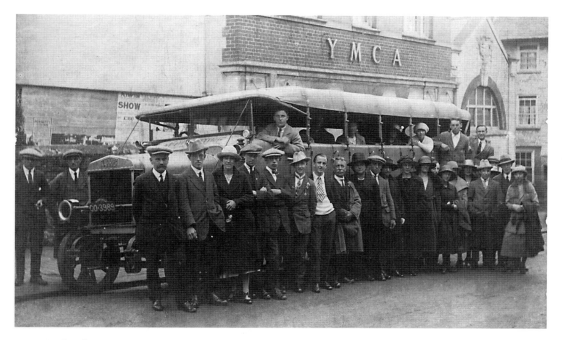

A charabanc party outside the YMCA building in Fore Street, *c.* 1925. The building was demolished in 1981 for road-widening purposes.

Above: The Saltash Volunteer Fire Brigade, 1919. Standing from left to right: W.J. Gardiner, G.H. Channings, J. Frost, B. Harvey, S. Rogers, J.H. Southern. Seated: W.W. Harvey (Second Officer), H.A. (Jim) Mace (Captain), J. Pickard (Sergeant).

Opposite above: One Saltash Home Guard platoon was based on Longlands School. Its members gathered there for a 'farewell' group photograph with their company commander, Capt. Stuart Rashleigh of Stoketon House, prior to the official Stand Down at the end of 1944.

Opposite below: At the 1952 Winkle Fair, 'King Cockle' was played by Trevor Solomon. Here he is threatening some young South Sea Islanders! To the left of His Majesty's cloak is the Court Jester played by Miss Ivy Train. Other notables present are the Mayor of Saltash, Councillor Miss Winifred M. Fearnside (behind the right-hand microphone – were they really 'live'?) and the Vicar of Saltash, Canon W.H. Prior (at right).

Members of the George Street Baptist Church Ambulance Corps, Plymouth, proceeding up Fore Street, Saltash, with their litter (a canopied stretcher on wheels), on 7 November 1913, when *en route* to Carkeel to collect a patient. (A useful reference point is today's Lloyds Bank at right-hand edge of photograph.) Local residents are obviously very interested in the proceedings!

Saltash Working Men's Club Band in 1938. There is a long tradition of musical groups of one kind and another in Saltash.

Lady Caradon, wife of Lord Caradon (formerly Sir Hugh Foot) reflects on some of the memorable occasions illustrated by photographs in her husband's study at their home, Trematon Castle in the 1970s.

Lady Caradon was a keen collector of antique fans, and here she indicates a special feature in one of the oldest and rarest fans in her collection.

five

Sporting Fixtures

Above: Saltash Town AFC team and officials, at the end of the 1930/31 season.

Opposite above: The Saltash YMCA football team and officials at the end of the 1919/20 season, during which they won the Cornwall Cup and Shield. Standing, from left to right: B. Dunn, N. Studden, W. Down, E. Wharton, E. Osborne, E. Jones, W. Goodman, R. Batten. Seated: D. Tookey, S. Goodman, L. Parkes, C. Vosper, R. Lucas, H. Cruttenden, W. Vosper. Front: E. Cruttenden, C. Screech.

Opposite below: Saltash United AFC team and officials, for the 1949/50 season.

Above: Members of Saltash Golf Club outside their clubhouse, *c.* 1936. Seated is the winner of the Page Cup, Mr H.C. Baker. The wooden building adjoined Church Road opposite St Stephen's School, (now Saltash College). The golf course extended over fields to the west and north, but it was closed when the Second World War began. Its former existence is now commemorated by a surfeit of modern road names (Fairway, Sunningdale Road, Birkdale Close, Carnoustie Drive, etc.)

Opposite above: Saltash Boys' School cricket team in 1938.

Opposite below: Members of the Saltash Cricket Club team, with umpire and scorer, in 1956.

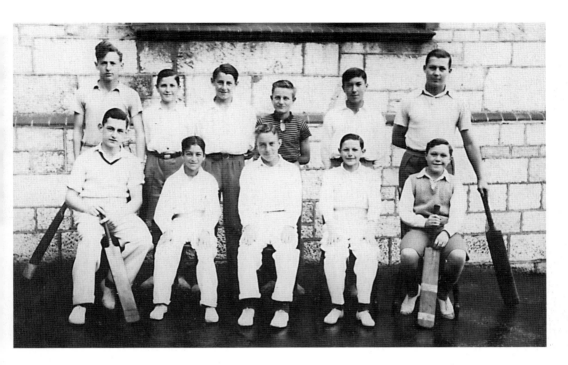

The long–distance runner David Bedford (former 10,000m world record holder) giving
encouragement to pupils at Saltash Comprehensive School in 1979.

Above: Pupils at Saltash Comprehensive School try to outrun David Bedford during his visit to the school in 1979!

Right: Ann Glanville (1796–1880). Of the many champion rowers produced by Saltash, the redoubtable Mrs Glanville was the most famous. Between 1830 and 1850 at regattas all over England, she and her crews of Saltash women were rarely beaten, even against male competitors. In 1842, Ann and her crew took their gig (by regular steamer services) to Le Havre, hoping to row against Frenchmen in the annual regatta there. However, for reasons of chivalry the French declined to compete and the Saltash women had to be content with winning a race against seamen from a British paddle steamer. So celebrated was Ann Glanville that legends regarding her exploits grew during her lifetime, and some accounts that have been written about her are fictitious. Nevertheless, she was a remarkable woman fully deserving her fame.

Above: Plenty of activity off Sand Quay beach during a Saltash Regatta, *c.* 1905. Two of the lady spectators have garlanded their hats.

Opposite above: Children from various Saltash schools assembled outside Longstone Junior School in 1974 to receive their Cycling Proficiency certificates from the Mayor, Councillor John Bryant.

Opposite below: Saltash Bowling Club members in their Golden Jubilee year, 1973. Back row, from left to right: Stanley Nichols, Frank Richard, Walter Lemin, Terry Steven, Frank Pollard, Charles Brown, Harold Jones, Arthur Coville, Charles Heal, Ted Thompson, Colin Wadge. Middle row: Pat O'Mahoney, Bill Heckford, Bill Maynard (Captain), Lance Parkes, Jack Prust, Phil Cann. Front row: Bill Hide, Jim Hosking, Charles Stephens, Brian Stephens, George Rogers.

Saltash Bowling Club members, *c.* 1950. Leo Gent, former manager of Daw's Creamery, is at the right-hand end of the middle row. In the front row, on the left, is the Revd H.E. Southgate, Vicar of Tideford.

Saltash County School hockey team, 1929.

six

Special Occasions

Fore Street, Saltash during King George V's Coronation celebrations in 1911. The crowd is awaiting the arrival of a procession. (On the right, the building with a just–visible projecting 'Tobacco & Cigars' sign is now the CLIC charity shop).

Peace Day, 1918 or 1919. A procession is about to enter the Baptist Chapel. Engadina Villas are the background.

Fore Street, decorated for the first revival of the ancient fair in August 1930. On the right an ice-cream cart is doing good business. On the left, below two dwellings, is J.H. Quick & Sons photographer's shop at No.51. Most of this block of properties was destroyed in the 1941 blitz.

The greengrocery and sweet shop of Mr Dale Stephens at No.60 Fore Street, decorated for the fair in August 1930.

Above: A procession in Fore Street to mark the Coronation of King George VI in 1937. Behind the mace bearer is the Mayor of Saltash, Alderman Ernest Webber, followed by his Deputy, Councillor Herbert J. Davy. All the properties shown are no more; the London Central Meat company's shop (at left) was opposite the Culver Road junction.

Opposite above: A civic procession in Fore Street, Saltash, headed by the Saltash Volunteer Fire Brigade, on King George VI's Coronation Day, 12 May 1937. The glass-panelled doors of the building in which the Brigade's engine was garaged can be seen in the middle background.

Opposite below: Trees were planted beside Callington Road near Kimberley Stadium to commemorate the Coronation in 1953. The Mayor of Saltash, Councillor Miss Winifred M. Fearnside MBE, was assisted by Mr Richard Heard (Borough Parks Superintendent) and the event was watched by Saltash Guides and Brownies. At a later date, the police station was built next to the trees.

Fore Street, blitzed. During the Second World War Saltash suffered considerable bombing by German planes and a number of people lost their lives.

A Service of Thanksgiving for Peace after the Second World War was held at the Longstone recreation field in 1945. On the platform, to the left, are the Mayor of Saltash, Alderman John F. Ashton, and his Deputy, Alderman Ernest Webber.

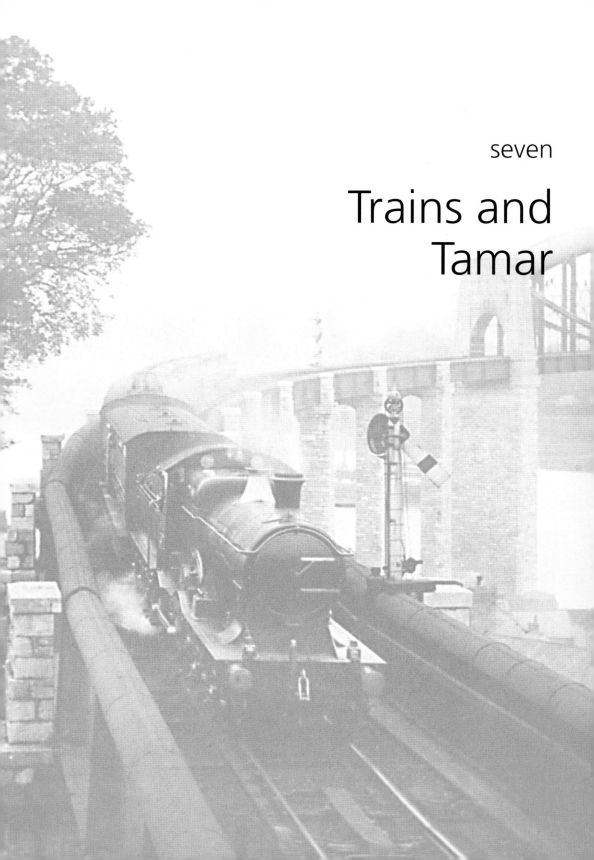

seven

Trains and Tamar

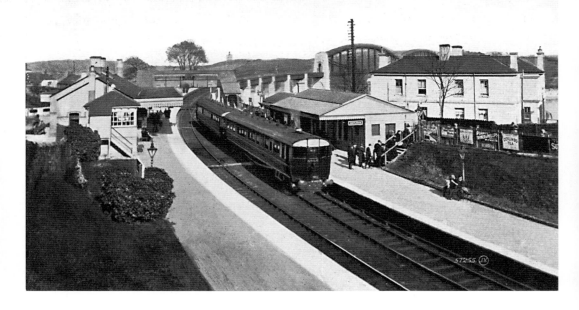

Railway Station, Saltash

Above: Saltash railway station, *c.* 1862. The siding in the foreground was later removed to make way for a larger building on the 'up' platform.

Opposite above: A train leaving the Royal Albert Bridge, *c.* 1905. John Paine, painter and decorator, utilised the side of his house, Marine Villa, to advertise his business to rail passengers. There is no record of how successful it was!

Opposite below: Saltash railway station, *c.* 1906. Just arrived is a train on the new Plymouth–Saltash suburban service which commenced in 1904. The trains were known as 'rail motors' or 'motor trains'; they were powered by steam engines situated within coaches. The footbridge was moved to a position in the foreground in 1908.

Isambard Kingdom Brunel's massive trestle viaduct across Coombe Creek, Saltash, in 1894 –
and nearing the end of its life. The masonry viaduct which superseded it can be seen behind,
almost completed, with derricks and a mobile steam crane upon it.

In 1906 the stone-arched bridge carrying Culver Road over the railway at Saltash station was
replaced by a steel structure having a greater span. These three photographs show stages in
the works.

A blasting operation to demolish the stone bridge at Saltash railway station.

The new steel bridge at Saltash railway station is in place in this photograph, and attracting huge attention.

A 'special' train at Saltash railway station, for the Royal Albert Bridge Centenary celebrations, 1 May 1959. Needless to say, the name of the fine steam locomotive was *Isambard Kingdom Brunel*.

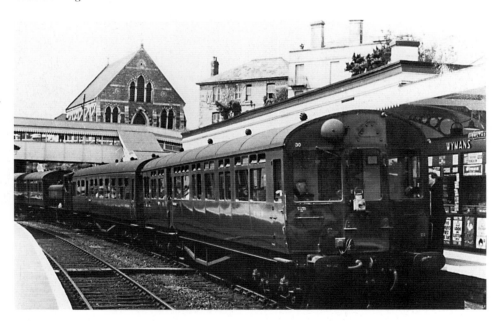

In the 1950s, the suburban rail service between Plymouth and Saltash reached its peak. Twenty-six trains per day ran in each direction, some of them crammed with 400 passengers. The opening of the Tamar Bridge in 1961 changed all that! Note the Wyman's bookstall on the platform, and the Baptist chapel in the background (erected in 1866, it was gutted by fire in 1987 and demolished in 1989).

eight

The Farming Scene

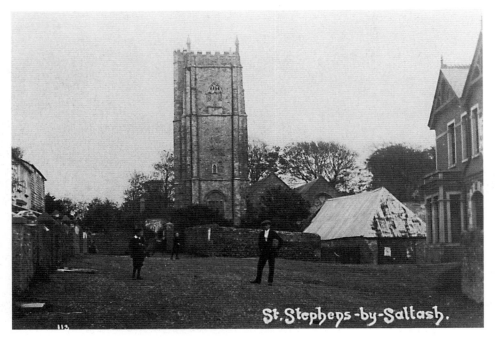

This view of St Stephen's from around 1925 includes, on the extreme right, the Cecil Arms, built in 1903 to replace the Church House Inn, which had been demolished in order to extend the churchyard. The nature of the road surface is typical of rural highways at that period.

The old granary at Shillingham, in St Stephen's parish. The granite straddle stones on which the building was raised prevented the entry of rats and mice.

Women and elderly persons needing 'self drive' transport favoured the tub-cart, as it was easy to board. In the south-west a tub-cart was called a 'jingle'. This pony and jingle, with owner John Ball, is pictured outside Skinham farmhouse (now the nucleus of the China Fleet Club) in 1919.

A double-horse hay sweep in operation at Hole Farm, St Stephen's parish in 1934.

The 'Auto Culto' cultivator was, in its day, at the cutting edge of technology! Here it is being operated by Mr Edgar Ball at Skinham, in 1939.

Cutting grass for hay with a popular Fordson tractor at Skinham Farm, St Stephen's parish in 1940. The man riding on the grass machine controlled the cutting operation.

Food production was a top priority on the home front in 1940. Here, Mr Arthur Ball is seen harvesting corn at Skinham Farm, in St Stephen's parish.

Farmer's daughter Phyllis Gregory raking hay at Higher Pill Farm, St Stephen's parish, in 1956. Farming was often a family affair, with wives and daughters playing their part alongside the men.

Above: The last collection of milk churns by lorry, 30 June 1978. Farmers put their churns of milk daily by the roadside, where full churns were collected and empty ones left for the next day. In 1978 all that changed when milk was collected by tankers which drove right into the farmyards, and churns became redundant. Now they often appear in auctions of farm bygones and are bought for both decoration and planting in gardens.

Right: Work on the land continues whatever the weather. A snow-covered farmyard at Higher Pill Farm in 1947; a year when there were far heavier than usual falls of snow in the south-west.

nine

Around the Neighbourhood

On the left in this 1910 view is Castle Park Quarry, one of eleven quarries in the Forder area which produced roadstone. It was the last one to be opened up, production having first commenced in the last decade of the nineteenth century. Some years after the quarry closed, the Castle Park Tea Gardens were laid out on the floor of the quarry.

Port Eliot, St German, seen here in around 1910 – the home of the Earls of St Germans. The core of the house is a remnant of a medieval priory. In 1564 the property was acquired by John Eliot, who concocted its name shortly afterwards. The eminent architect, Sir John Soane, designed a large extension, which was commenced in 1802. Behind is the finest Norman church in Cornwall.

Above: A party of members of Launceston Old Cornwall Society visiting St German's church in the 1970s.

Right: The magnificent Norman doorway of St German's church. The designs of the stonework are typical of the period and can be seen on some other Norman buildings in Cornwall.

Above: The rear garden of Port Eliot. From its appearance, this could at one time have been a bowling green.

Above: Landulph church, seen from across the daffodil fields. This is an area largely given over to the growing of daffodils and narcissi, the Du Plessis family being well-known growers in the area.

Left: Literally 'roses round the door' outside this cottage at Ince.

Opposite below: Dando and his dogs: A medieval misericord in St German's church, commemorating the legend of Dando, one of the monks of St German's Priory, who was not faithful to his vows and kept company with those who enjoyed 'the good things of life'. This included hunting and drinking freely of wine. One Sunday morning while hunting at Erth Barton, near St Germans, Dando had an encounter with Satan and came to an unpleasant end. His companions were so affected by the incident that many of them went to live in the priory and thenceforth devoted their lives to God and the Church. This misericord is the only part of the furnishings of the priors' choir which survives. The choir was demolished in the Dissolution of the Monasteries. Dando, with his hounds, is carrying his game on the stock of his crossbow, which rests on his shoulder.

Ince Castle, a sixteenth-century manor house once lived in by a member of the Killigrew family. It has four corner towers with pointed tent roofs, joined on one side by a parapet over a doorway at the top of a flight of steps. Local legend has it that Killigrew kept four wives in the four towers, each locked up so that none should have knowledge of the others!

Ince Castle was once the home of a shipping magnate. It is built of red brick, which is unusual for such a building in Cornwall.

The stable at Ince Castle is adorned with the nameplate from the Great Western Railway steam locomotive *Ince Castle*, one of the famous 'Castle' class of engines.

The engine nameplate on the stable at Ince Castle.

The ancient clapper bridge over the River Lynher at Pillaton. Such bridges were built entirely of large slabs of stone.

The Norman keep at Trematon Castle, and the Georgian house built within what is left of the old enclosing walls of the castle. The house was for many years the home of Lord and Lady Caradon, and the latter, a great animal lover, is seen in the photograph taking a bowl of water to a guest's dog in a car.

Early morning mist filters the spring sunshine on the grounds of Trematon Castle. The grounds and garden are beautifully laid out, with rose beds surrounding a formal garden and lawn in front of the house. A bust of Homer set on a pedestal can be seen on the lower lawn.

The gate tower at Trematon Castle, built by the Black Prince, and showing the window of the room in which the Black Prince is said to have slept.

St Dominick church. The church is sheltered by beech trees and its tower is remarkable for its overhanging top, resting on a corbel table. The lower part of the tower is thirteenth-century. The top was added in the fifteenth century and the old parapet embodied into it.

Burraton Cross. The shop of F. Hearl, saddler and harness maker can be seen here in 1910. The mouth of Liskeard Road was widened in about 1937 by the removal of the properties at the left-hand edge. Traffic lights were installed at the crossroads in 1962 and it is now a very busy junction.

Stoketon House in St Stephen's parish was built in the Gothic revival style towards the end of the eighteenth century by Stephen Drew. For most of the nineteenth century, it was owned by the De Courcy family (including the 32nd and 33rd Barons Kinsale). In 1901 the house was purchased by the Rashleigh family who lived there until 1958 (the date of this photograph). It was gutted by fire in 1984 and subsequently demolished.

A pedigree South Devon cow is proudly displayed at Bush Farm, Pillaton in 1908. Bush Farm was in St Stephen's parish until 1894, when parish boundary changes put it into Pillaton parish.

Above: In this view of Antony Passage, the building on the extreme left was once the Ferry House Inn, which closed in 1921, some ten years before this picture was taken. The ferry was of medieval origin and ceased operating in 1952.

Opposite above: The construction of Ince Castle was commenced by Henry Killigrew around 1640 and completed by Edward Nosworthy in about 1655. Originally known as Ince House, it was designed as a dwelling in 'mock castle' form (although coincidentally it did play a part in the Civil War of 1642–46). From the mid-nineteenth century, the building served as a farmhouse. In 1920 it was restored by the Hon. Montagu Elliot. Further extensive refurbishment was commenced in 1960 by the first Viscount Boyd of Merton (Alan Lennox-Boyd, Colonial Secretary 1954-59).

Opposite below: Many villages had their own bands and much local talent surfaced as young men were keen to join them. This is Trematon brass band, pictured in around 1905.

Workers at Jefford's Tor quarry, Burraton Coombe, *c.* 1920. Mr Sam Jefford, one of the brothers who owned the business, is standing behind the wagon. After crushing, the blue elvan stone (used in road construction) was conveyed by tramway to quays at Forder Creek, where it was loaded into sailing vessels. Tor Quarry closed in 1964.

Curious double gravestones in the cemetery at Saltash. The deceased was married twice, and after his demise, each of his wives erected their own stones. The one on the right has letters unusually carved in relief.

Above left: A garden feature which causes much interest is a green letterbox in a garden in Culver Road.

Above right: The boundary stone of the Saltash Turnpike Trust still stands near a junction in Culver Road. The Turnpike Trusts were disbanded in the late 1870s.

Opposite above: In the late 1980s, a tunnel was constructed to ease traffic congestion as part of the new Saltash bypass, and was opened in 1988. It is quarter of a mile long and was excavated mainly through Upper Devonian slate. This model of work in progress is loaned by Saltash Town Council. A pilot tunnel, visible top right, was completed in 1986. It was then enlarged to full size using the 40-ton boring machine seen here.

Opposite below: By arrangement with the contractors, Messrs Balfour Beatty, a public viewing of the tunnel was held on Sunday 4 September 1988, twelve days before it was opened to traffic. Leading the first 'walk through' was Mr Robert Hicks MP, flanked by the Chairman of Caradon District Council, Councillor Alfred Brooking (left) and the Mayor of Saltash, Councillor John Scannell (right). In 2003 the tunnel was plagued with problems including cracks in the walls and water seepage, and lengthy repair work was undertaken to restore it to its original state.

Other local titles published by Tempus

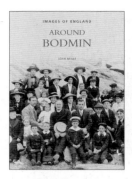

Bodmin

JOHN NEALE

Illustrated with 200 images, many never before published, this selection charts many changes which have taken place in the Cornish town of Bodmin in times of both war and peace over the last 100 years. Photographs of shops which have ceased trading and buildings that have been demolished feature alongside vistas of great houses, churches, the railway, Bodmin Gaol and timeless Bodmin Moor. Local people are also remembered; craftsmen, sportsmen, the police, fire brigade, soldiers and even a one-time bank robber.

0 7524 3054 8

Folklore of Cornwall

TONY DEANE AND TONY SHAW

This volume touches on the wide variety of legends, songs and stories unique to Cornwall and their relationship with the rugged landscape; from standing stones and tales of sea-monsters and mermaids to ghosts, fairies and giants. The book looks at pagan ceremonies and old traditions, and the very Cornish love of singing. It further discusses the Cornish tongue, and of course no study of Cornwall would be complete without some consideration of King Arthur and his legacy upon the folklore of the county.

0 7524 2929 9

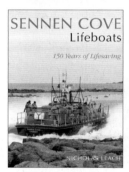

Sennen Cove Lifeboats 150 Years of Lifesaving

NICHOLAS LEACH

Considered one of the most treacherous areas of Britain's coastline, Land's End has seen many shipwrecks over the past two thousand years. In 1853, the RNLI established a lifeboat station at nearby Sennen Cove and the people of this small Cornish village have been saving lives and helping those in distress ever since. Nicholas Leach tells the story of Sennen's lifeboats and the volunteer crews who have manned them in this, the first comprehensive history of the lifeboats and wrecks off the tip of Cornwall.

0 7524 3111 0

Truro History & Guide

CHRISTINE PARNELL

Truro has variously been the commercial, industrial and spiritual heart of Cornwall throughout its long and varied history, despite the many hardships and setbacks it has suffered, from the ravages of the Black Death in the fourteenth century to the Civil War in the seventeenth. The building of the cathedral and bestowing of city status on the market town confirmed Truro's importance and, as such, it is now the administrative centre of Cornwall.

0 7524 2640 0

If you are interested in purchasing other books published by Tempus, or in case you have difficulty finding any Tempus books in your local bookshop, you can also place orders directly through our website

www.tempus-publishing.com

or from **BOOKPOST**, Freepost, PO Box 29, Douglas, Isle of Man, IM99 1BQ
tel 01624 836000   email bookshop@enterprise.net